DRUMSTICK**C**

L

a realistic approach to snare drum technique applied to drumset

Jeff Moore

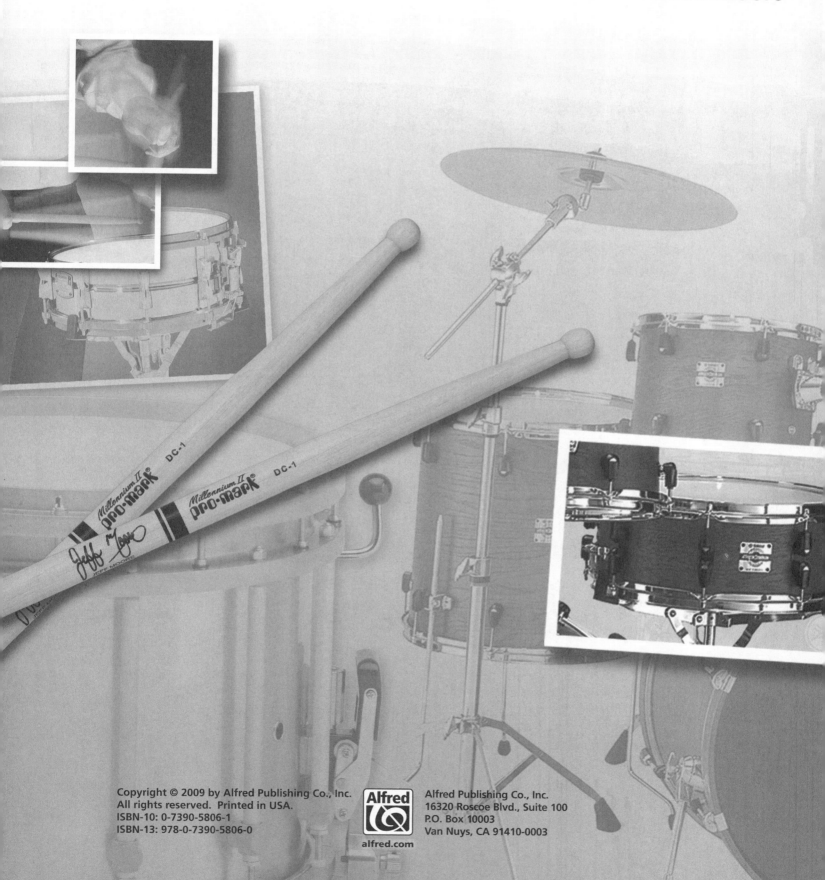

Alfred

alfred.com

Alfred Publishing Co., Inc.
16320 Roscoe Blvd., Suite 100
P.O. Box 10003
Van Nuys, CA 91410-0003

Table of Contents

Dedication

I dedicate this book to all my students. It was the path to discovery that we shared that provided the motivation and foundation to the methods and approaches in this book. To those of us who teach, study and pursue total percussion education and the transfer value of this huge family of instruments, I submit these ideas for your consideration.

To my parents, Harry and Sue Ann Moore, who encouraged me and supported my passion for drumming and music, even though I knew at times they were concerned where it might eventually lead me. They trusted in me and fostered my ambitions and I will never be able to repay them for the opportunities and support they provided.

To my wife Mindy, who for the last two decades has been my source of inspiration, encouragement and security that has allowed me to pursue my career goals without compromise. Her unwavering support throughout my touring, travels, practicing and performance has made all the difference in my ability to achieve the things that I set out to do. Her love and patience fuels my desire to continue this lifelong pursuit and is the centering force in my life.

Personal Acknowledgements

I owe a debt of gratitude to all my teachers who helped steer me in the right direction throughout my career. My percussion teachers were: Forrest Elledge, Galen Lemmon, Anthony Cirone, Ralph Hardimon, Glen Crosby, Dr. Robert Schietroma, Ron Fink, Chris Thompson and James Latimer.

The opportunity to learn and to teach provided by Scott Stewart in my 11 years with the Madison Scouts Drum and Bugle Corps has had an incredible influence on my life and teaching. Scott is among the finest people I know and I, like most of the staff and members who passed through the Scout organization during his tenure, owe him a great deal for the positive impact he has had on our lives. I have never known a more selfless, caring and loving individual in my life. The Scout percussion staff, specifically Dan Neimeyer, Jeff Peterson, Mark Tarrant, Taras Nahirniak, Clif Walker, Jim Atkinson, Jim Yakas, Jeff Spanos and Brian Johnson, all had a tremendously positive impact on me, and proved to be a great "sounding board" for many of the ideas contained in this book.

My colleagues and peers have also contributed to my ability and knowledge through their own pursuits and their willingness to share their ideas. My friends and fellow students Dr. Robert Bridge, Kennan Wylie, Steve MacDonald, Jon Lee, Jim Riley and Pat Fitzgerald all had a great influence on my understanding of percussion. Dr. Ney Rosauro, Dr. Doug Walter, Professor Gary Cook, Dr. Steven Hemphill, Dr. Richard Greenwood, Dr. Johnny Pherigo and Professor Kirk Gay continue to be great sources of information, friendship and support.

The company support I enjoy is truly remarkable and it would prove difficult, if not impossible, to experience all I have without their superior products and support. Maury Brochstein, Staci Stokes and everyone at Pro-Mark; John Wittmann, Dennis DeLucia, Dino Riccio and Joel Tetzlaff at Yamaha; Johnny Lee Lane, Bruce Jacoby at Remo; Erik Paiste and Ed Clift at Paiste; and Memo Acevedo and Steve Nigohosian at Latin Percussion.

Project Acknowledgements

I wish to thank Dave Black, Steve Houghton and everyone at Alfred Publishing for believing in the book and for supporting the project throughout its development. To those ends, I would also like to thank Ray Brych and Rick Gratton who through great patience and perseverance helped me to complete this book and assisted greatly in the concept and editing process.

Finally, I wish to thank Professor James Petercsak for the initial idea for this project and for personally selecting me and believing I was the right person for the job. So many in the percussion world owe "J.P." so much for what he has done on their behalf and I am privileged to be one of the hundreds that owe him more than they can ever repay.

Inspiration for the Book

The material in this book grew largely out of books that have come before. As with any body of knowledge, each time the material is revisited, new insights and ideas come to light. The concepts, foundations and some of the exercises contained within owe their existence to these books that came before. I highly recommend these books and the knowledge they contain as you pursue your percussion skills.

Stick Control –
George Lawrence Stone

Master Studies –
Joe Morello

Teaching Percussion (3rd edition) –
Gary Cook

Savage Rudimental Workshop –
Matt Savage

Drumset Control –
Marvin Dahlgren

The New Breed –
Gary Chester

Linear Time Playing –
Gary Chaffee

Jeff Moore, Orlando, Florida 2008

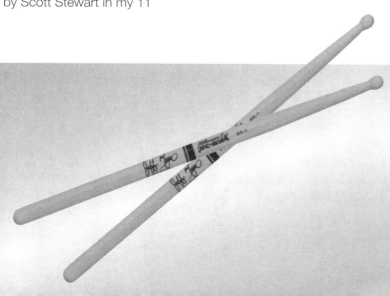

PREFACE
Fundamental Drumstick Control

The "Hands-Separate Approach" is a different concept applied to a traditional method. Most percussionists learn arm, wrist and finger coordination one hand at a time. Many teachers determined that a student focusing on one limb at a time could more easily scrutinize the technical elements involved in stroke production. Beginning students usually start playing a single stroke with the right hand. The instructions focus the student's attention on elements of grip, hand position, motion, stick height, volume and sound quality. After suitable improvement through repetition, the student is introduced to the same concepts in the left hand. Ordinarily, the student combines the two motions into the single-stroke roll. Many beginning exercises focus the student's concentration on reading rhythmic partials, holding a consistent tempo and keeping accurate spacing of the rhythms within the pulse. Although all of these elements are crucial to early development, a critical element is missed.

The hands-separate motion and *feeling* that the student was initially perfecting is not focused on, utilized or referenced in the teaching of the hands-together pattern. The student, instead, receives specific corrections related to individual technical inconsistencies, such as a change in grip, height, sound quality, etc. In most cases, once both limbs begin to move simultaneously, a fundamental change in the way the player feels and controls the motion changes. To experience this phenomenon, try this exercise: First, slowly move your right arm up and down from the elbow, like you are waving with your hand, using your arm and not your wrist. Notice how natural, normal and comfortable this movement is. Next, slowly move your left hand side to side from the elbow, like you are wiping a table. Notice again how easy this movement is to execute and how relaxed the rest of your muscles are. Finally, very slowly, do both these

movements simultaneously. These relatively simple movements can become frustrating when trying to do them together.

This natural lack of independence can be one of the most critical skills in the development of a drummer, yet no beginning method book discusses or offers an approach to improve this essential skill. In fact, many beginning books contain combination after combination of stickings that can exacerbate the problem by frustrating the student as each new combination brings the student a feeling of "starting over" from the beginning. In drumset books such as Gary Chester's *The New Breed* or mallet books such as Leigh Howard Stevens' *Method of Movement*, exercises and strategies for gaining greater independence are presented, but are considered advanced techniques. Fundamental independence exercises at the beginning stages of development can aid in a student's snare drum progress, while also providing a base of muscle facility valuable in approaching other percussion instruments.

Transfer Value

Transfer value is a term used to describe movements or concepts common between the different instruments in the percussion family. A solid snare drum facility transfers physical strength and coordination benefits to the other percussion instruments. In addition, if snare drum practice is approached from the independence method, then there are mental concepts that transfer from snare drum as well. Common concepts and skill sets exist between seemingly different instruments in the percussion family. For example, if one learns to play a paradiddle on snare drum utilizing the independence method, a single-hand ostinato is continuously repeated, and then slowly and sequentially the opposite hand is added to complete the rudiment.

Single Paradiddle

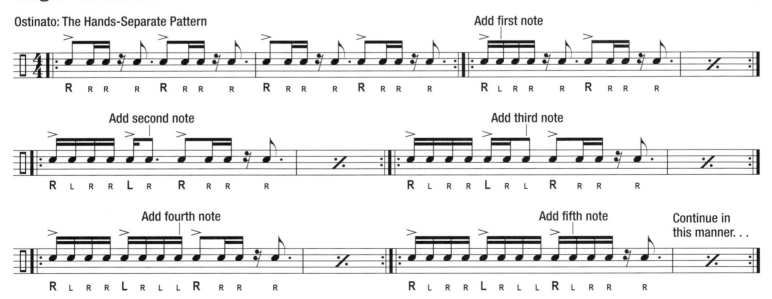

This "step-by-step" approach is similar to the one utilized when building a new time pattern on drumset. It also lays the foundation for linear drumming by establishing a "two-limb" approach[1]. This concept also has a parallel in the genre of marimba, where a single-hand ostinato is performed in the left hand (bass line), while the right hand performs a melody with different

---

[1] The term "linear" means no two limbs are playing notes simultaneously. For an excellent method to build this facility, Russ Miller's book, *Transitions*, (from Alfred) is highly recommended.

rhythmic and pitch content. This level of independence is required in most intermediate to advanced four-mallet literature. The transfer value of this particular concept to the other instruments is profound.

It is crucial to introduce the independence method as early as possible and that is the primary motivation for this book. The concepts, exercises and ideas presented in this book are offered in the spirit of introducing students to a faster way to develop technical control over their muscle groups (coordination), and a method to quickly gain sticking facility and vocabulary.

The Muscle Groups

Arm
The stroke starts from the shoulder, travels through the lifted elbow and wrist, then "whips" the stick onto the head.

Wrist
The wrist lever is utilized for accented and unaccented notes and requires a great deal of isolation.

Finger
The final lever, the fingers, is usually employed for unaccented notes and rebound control for multiple strokes. Understanding that we use accented and unaccented notes to phrase on percussion instruments, and that the majority of notes played are unaccented, it is curious why this lever can appear so underdeveloped. Given the difficulty and relative weakness of the non-writing hand's finger-stroke muscles, much of stick technique practice time should be spent working this lever. In most cases it's not worked enough, if at all. It is usually the last lever to be worked on, and many times it is not isolated properly for the student to understand how to practice and use this lever. Given a moderate tempo, roll, diddle and flam passages will utilize this lever. The faster the tempo and rhythmic content, the more control and strength are needed in the fingers. With sensitive concert snare drumming, general technique and rolling on timpani, pianissimo triangle performance, etc., the need for finger dexterity is clear. Part of any comprehensive technique program should give regular attention to the isolation and growth of the finger stroke.

Percussion Strokes

Stick movement (stroke technique) can be named and described in many ways. Regardless of the name, it is important to practice each of the stroke types listed below separately in order to put them together successfully:

Stroke Type	Other Names	Description
1. Full	Natural, Rebound, Legato	Start the stroke from any height (usually high), play and return to the same position. Avoid jabbing with the forearm or pulling the stick back with your wrist. Let the stick "rebound naturally."
2. Tap	Low, Unaccented, Soft	Start the stroke from a low (close to the drumhead) position, play and return to the same low position. It is an exclusively low version of the "full" stroke.
3. Down	Controlled, Staccato	Start the stroke high, play and stop the stick close to the drumhead.
4. Up	Lift, Tap-lift	Start the stroke low, play and end by lifting the tip to a high position.
5. Double	Roll Strokes, Drags, Open Rolls, Diddles	Start the stroke from any height, play the first stroke and allow the stick to rebound (usually to a slightly lower height than the first). Play the second stroke (if needed, increase velocity of the second stroke to make both strokes sound even) and return to the original height of the first stroke. **At extremely fast speeds and/or soft dynamics:** Play a controlled bounce of two notes.
6. Triple	3's, French Rolls	**At a slower speed:** Start the stroke from any height, play the first stroke and allow the stick to rebound (usually to a slightly lower height than the first), allow the second stroke to be played from the energy (bounce) provided by the first stroke, play the third stroke (if needed, increase velocity of the third stroke to make it sound even) and return to the original height of the first stroke. **At a faster speed:** A controlled bounce of three notes, the stick is lifted up after the third note.
7. Multiple Bounce	Buzz, Concert Rolls, Closed	Start at any height; allow each stroke to bounce as long as possible. Notice the amount of finger pressure used for each length. Avoid the temptation to remove the middle finger from the stick.

Metronome Games

This is a concept in which the individual moves the click of the metronome or drum machine away from the downbeat. One method of how this can be achieved is by eliminating one of the partials from a beat. In duple meter this creates a 3/8 or 3/16 bar, depending on the sub-division the student is working with. It can be achieved in triple meter by giving one beat either 2 or 4 partials to move the click mentally. This rhythmic displacement, when practiced in conjunction with fewer clicks per bar, helps make the student increasingly more responsible for larger amounts of space. This will ultimately improve the student's rhythmic timing and sense of pulse.

How to Use the Book

This book is divided into sections to isolate stroke types. Stroke-type exercises are presented separately in duple and triple meter, and then mixing both meters. Each stroke type is presented and should be practiced in three steps:

1. The "Hands-Separate" pattern, giving the player the opportunity to establish the movement and sound as a model for the performance of any "Hands-Together" pattern.

2. The "Hands-Together" pattern is then built by incrementally adding the opposite hand to the "Hands-Separate" pattern. Independence exercises will help with the coordination of this step.

3. The complete "Hands-Together" pattern is presented and executed without the build-up. To assess that the player is utilizing the same movement and sound as found in the "Hands-Separate" pattern, it is recommended that the student perform the "Hands-Together" patterns on two different sounding surfaces so that each hand pattern can easily be scrutinized.

Rhythmic Ratios

The exercises in this book will be written in several different rhythmic notations. This will help the student become familiar with different rhythmic values. To aid in understanding, initial exercises are presented in several rhythmic ratios. The intent is that the student develops a stronger sense of rhythmic subdivision by experiencing the same rhythmic ratio notated in different ways.

Focus Concepts

1. The ratios (hand-to-hand speed) in some of the exercises are identical. Only the rhythmic notation is different.

2. The rhythmic notation impacts the relationship of the rhythm relative to tempo (metronome mark), but not the hand-to-hand ratio. Therefore, 32nd notes are no more difficult ratio wise than eighth notes. It is the tempo, if fast enough, that can make the 32nds more challenging. Conversely, quarter-note triplets to eighth-note triplets are no more difficult ratio wise than eighth-note triplets to sixteenth-note triplets. Whether written in simple meter (4/4) or compound meter (12/8, 6/8), the rhythm ratios are the same.

3. Try playing on two different sound surfaces so you can listen to the lead hand in isolation while performing "Hands Together."

4. Count the rhythms out loud while playing the exercises. Notice how the rhythms from your voice "fit in" or "line-up" with your hands.

Chapter 1
Accented Single Strokes

single-stroke accent to tap – (hands separate)

The term *Bucks* is a name rudimental drummers use to describe a
common exercise consisting of one accent, followed by one tap.

Bucks

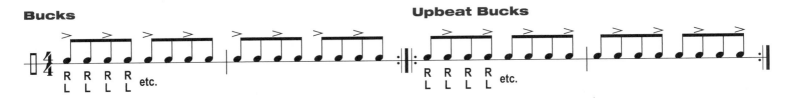

Upbeat Bucks

Triple Bucks

Quadruple Bucks

Both Hands in Unison (Double Stops) — Bucks

Both Hands in Unison (Double Stops) — Triple Bucks

Both Hands in Unison (Double Stops) — Quadruple Bucks

Bucks — Build Up

single-stroke accent to tap – (hands separate continued)

Double Accent Permutation

Accent Add On

Bucks and Triple Bucks Combined (5, 7 and 10)

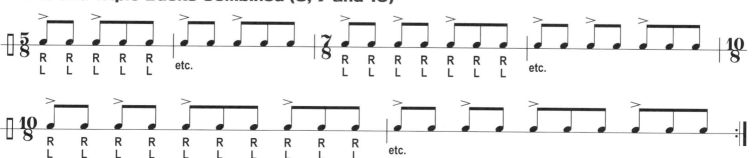

accented single-stroke builders – (independence approach)

Accent Single-Stroke Builder — Bucks Track 2

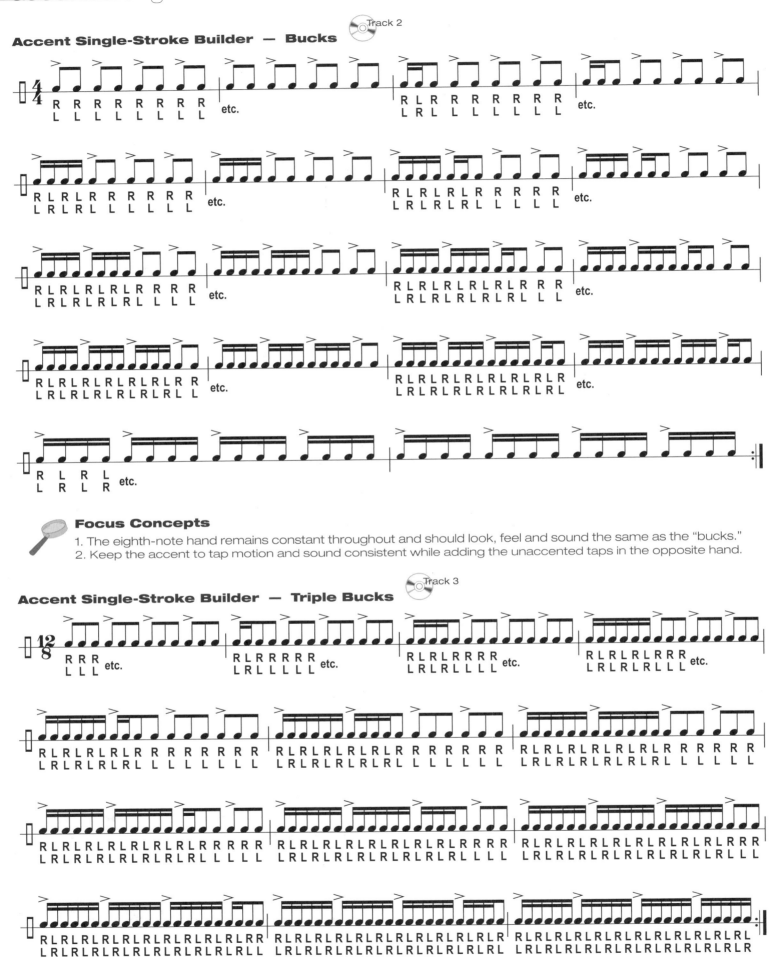

Focus Concepts

1. The eighth-note hand remains constant throughout and should look, feel and sound the same as the "bucks."
2. Keep the accent to tap motion and sound consistent while adding the unaccented taps in the opposite hand.

Accent Single-Stroke Builder — Triple Bucks Track 3

accented single-stroke builders – (independence approach continued)

Accent Single-Stroke Builder — Quadruple Bucks   Track 4

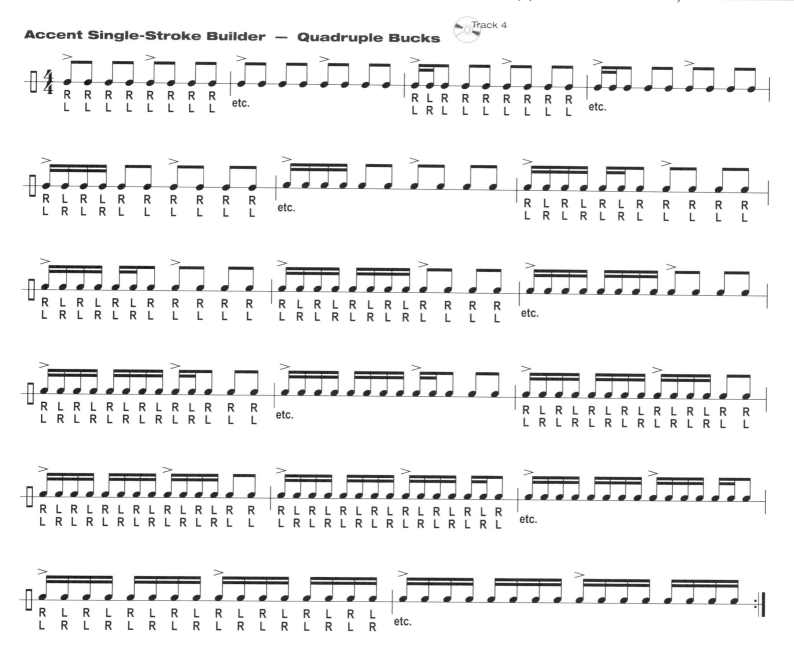

This exercise starts with Triple Bucks in the right hand and Bucks in the left, and then it reverses. The result is a polyrhythm (two or more rhythms sounded simultaneously). In this case, it is a 3:2 or 3 with 2 polyrhythm.

Independence Building   Track 5

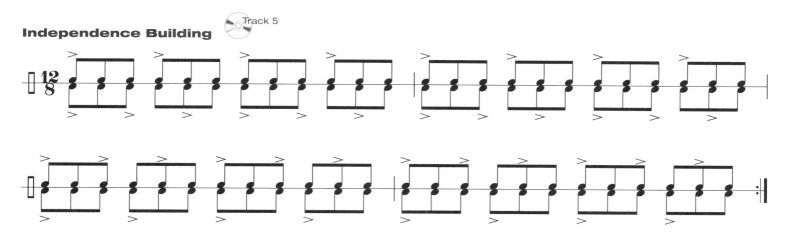

accented single-stroke builders – (independence approach continued)

Bucks with 5, 7 and 10 Track 6

NOTE: Also play reversing the hands.

Independence Building (Ostinato & Quarter Notes)

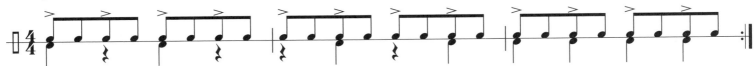

Independence Building (Ostinato & Eighth Notes)

Independence Building (Ostinato & Sixteenth Notes) Track 7

Independence Building (Triplets — Single Notes)

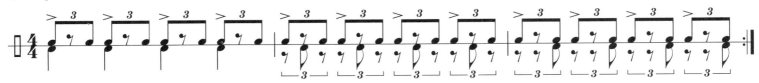

Independence Building (Triplets — Two Notes) Track 8

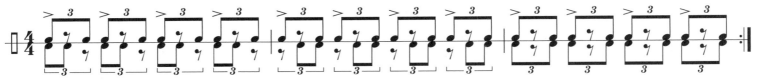

accented single-stroke roll – (independence approach)

Accented Single-Stroke Roll Builder (Eighths to Sixteenths)

Accented Single-Stroke Roll Builder (Sixteenths to 32nds)

Accented Single-Stroke Roll Builder (Triplets to Sextuplets)

accented single strokes – (building up common figures)

Focus Concepts

1. Any "hands-together" rhythm can be broken down to the "hands-separate" pattern.
2. Break down any "hands-together" rhythm by playing each hand on a different sound surface to hear the "hands-separate" pattern.

Track 9

Sixteenth-Note Common Accent Schemes (Bucks)

Sixteenth-Note Common Accent Schemes (Upbeat Bucks)

Track 10

Sixteenth-Note Common Accent Schemes (Triple Bucks)

Sixteenth-Note Common Accent Schemes (Quadruple Bucks)

accented single strokes – (building up common figures continued)

Sixteenth-Note Common Accent Schemes #1 (Multiple Accents)

Sixteenth-Note Common Accent Schemes #2 (Multiple Accents)

Sixteenth-Note Common Accent Schemes #3 (Multiple Accents)

Sixteenth-Note Common Accent Schemes #4 (Multiple Accents)

Sixteenth-Note Common Accent Schemes #5 (Triple Bucks Displaced)

accented single strokes — (building up common figures continued)

accented single strokes – (building up common figures
— triple rhythm continued)

Common Accent Scheme #5 (Polyrhythmic Accents, Triple Bucks & Bucks)

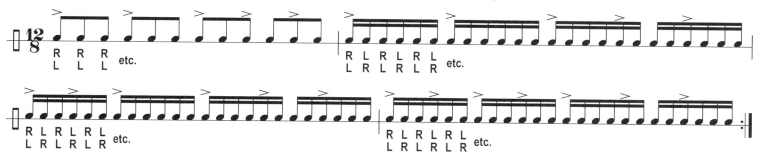

Common Accent Scheme #6 (Polyrhythmic Accents)

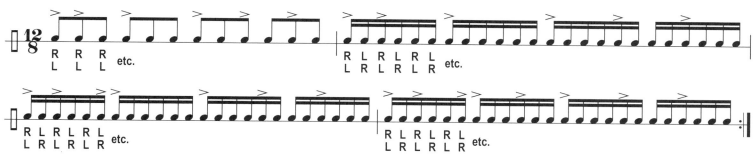

Common Accent Scheme #7 (Polyrhythmic Accents)

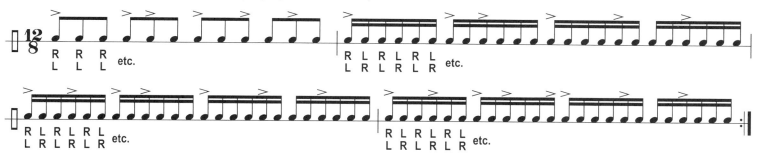

Common Accent Scheme #8 (Polyrhythmic Accents)

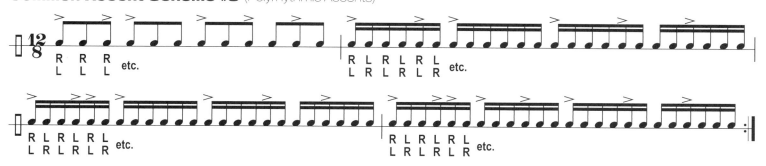

Common Accent Scheme #9 (Polyrhythmic Accents, Triple Bucks & Bucks)

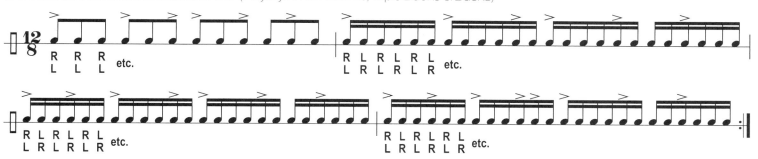

accented single-strokes triplets – ("swing" bucks)

 Focus Concepts

1. Another way to utilize the "hands-separate approach" when playing accented triplet rhythms is to break the "hands-separate pattern" down hand-to-hand. This produces "swing bucks."
2. Practice these exercises as written and then move, add and subtract accents to make new accent "schemes."

Swing Bucks

Swing Bucks (Fill-in the Triplets)   Track 13

Swing Bucks (Notated in Sextuplets)

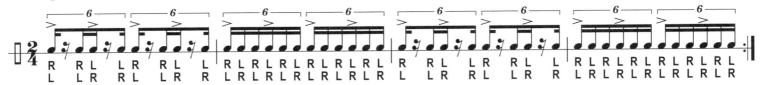

Upbeat Swing Bucks

Upbeat Swing Bucks (Fill-in the Triplets)   Track 14

Upbeat Swing Bucks (Notated in Sextuplets)

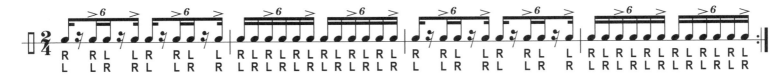

accented single strokes – (the grids)

The *Grid* is a name rudimental drummers have given to an exercise that moves (displaces) accents within a rudiment or sticking combination. Since rudiments are commonly found in three- or four-part elements, triple- and duple-based accent exercises provide a helpful template.

The following eight exercises show the most common one- and two-accent patterns and are arranged in a standard 4-2-1 structure. 4-2-1 refers to the number of accents an individual plays before moving the accent(s) over. Learn

these exercises as written, and in subsequent chapters we will layer rudiments over these accent structures. When we do, we adjust the order of elements within the rudiment, creating new technical combinations (what your hands are physically doing) and mental combinations (what your brain is thinking in relation to the pulse). Learn and memorize them to make their utilization comfortable. Practice with a metronome and count quarter notes out loud while playing these accent schemes. Tap your foot on quarter notes as well.

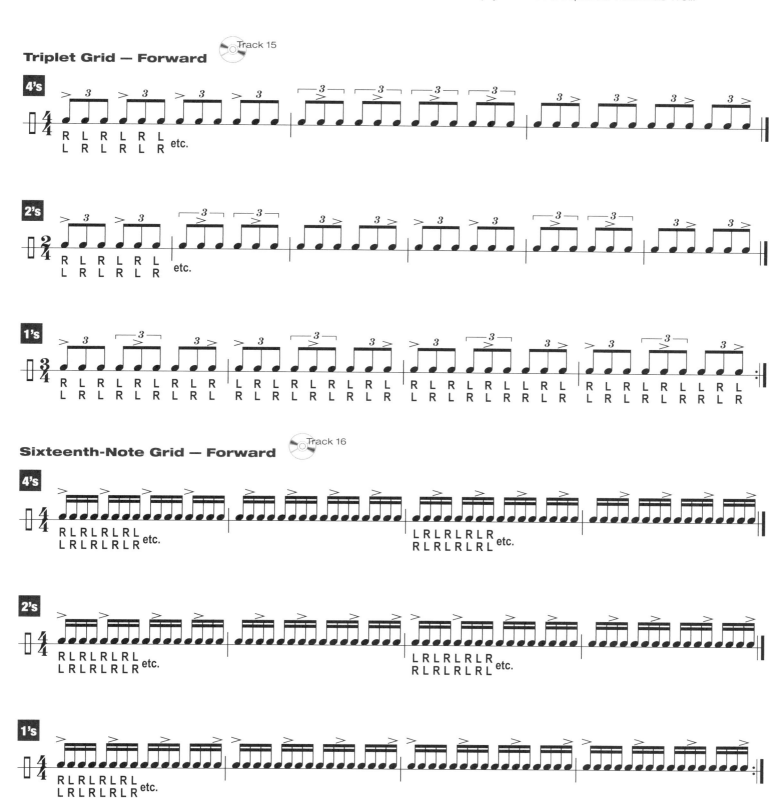

accented single strokes – (the grids continued)

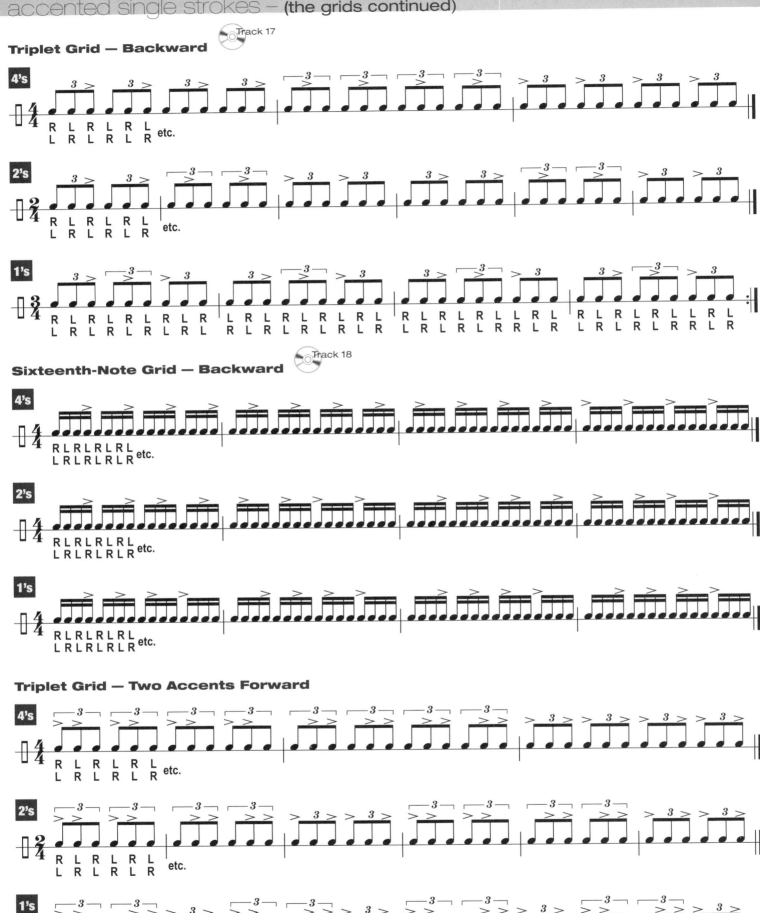

accented single strokes – (the grids continued)

Sixteenth-Note Grid — Two Accents Forward

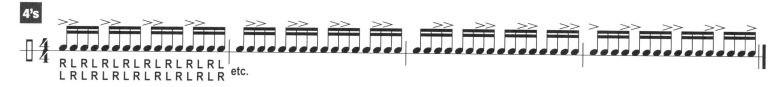

Triplet Grid — Two Accents Backward

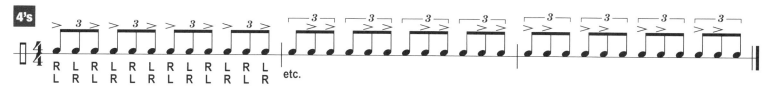

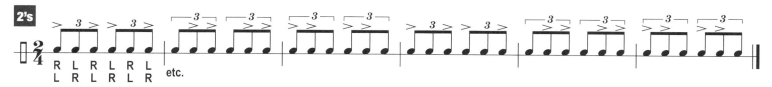

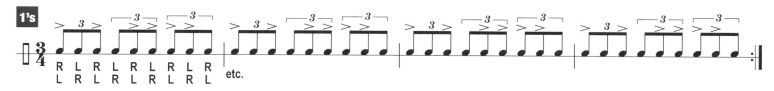

Sixteenth-Note Grid — Two Accents Backward

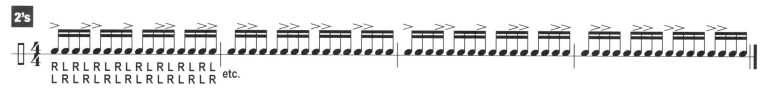

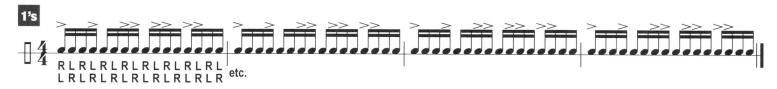

accented single strokes (duple and triple combinations)

Track 19

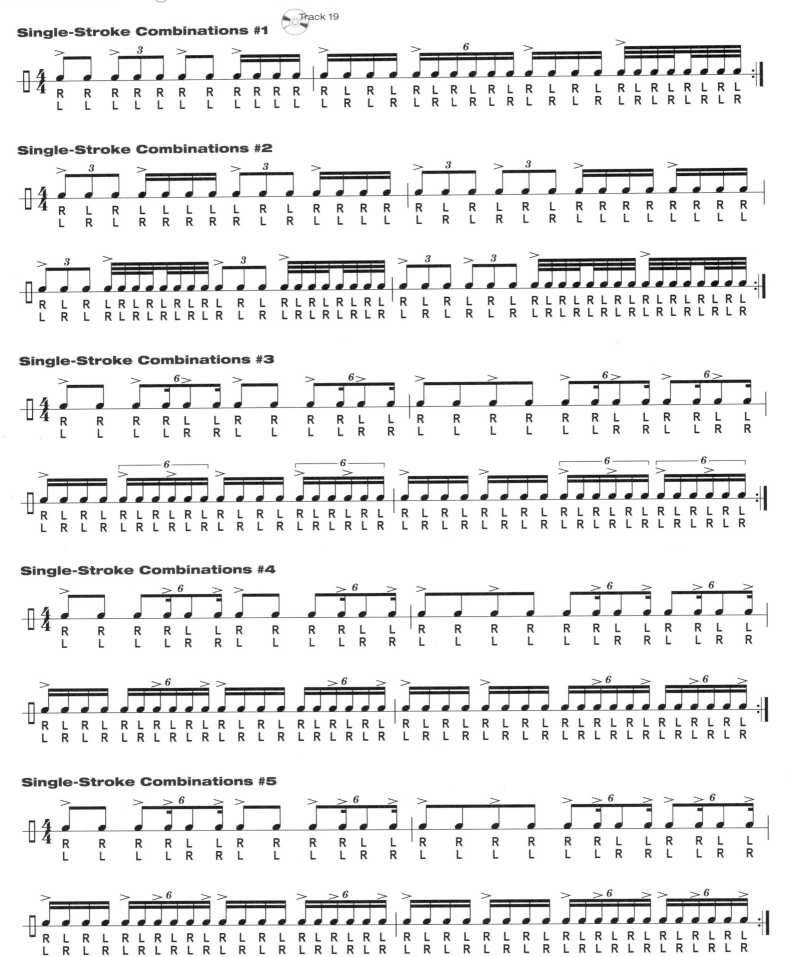

accented single strokes (drumset applications — time functioning)

Drumset Legend

Note: ✗ is commonly used for cymbals rather than ♩ to further distinguish them from drums.

Independence Building (Ostinato and Sixteenth Ghost Notes)   Track 20

Independence Building (Ostinato and Eighth Notes, Reggae/Ska Beat)   Track 21

Bass Drum Patterns Play each with the hand patterns above.

Independence Building with Triplets (Single Notes/Shuffle-Beat Variations)   Track 22

Independence Building with Triplets (Two Notes/Jazz-Time Variations)   Track 23

accented single strokes (drumset applications — fills & solos)

Track 24

Bucks Fill Idea — RH Clockwise   **Bucks Fill Idea — LH Counterclockwise**

Track 25

Accent the Upbeats — RH Clockwise   **Accent the Upbeats — LH Counterclockwise**

Track 26

Triplets — LH Counterclockwise   **Triplets — RH Clockwise**

Track 27

Triplets Clockwise — Two-Bar Phrase

Track 28

Triple Bucks Clockwise — Sixteenth Notes   **Triple Bucks Counterclockwise — Sixteenth Notes**

Chapter 2
Accented Double Strokes

accent to double stroke (hands separate)

Huck-a-Bucks

Upbeat Huck-a-Bucks

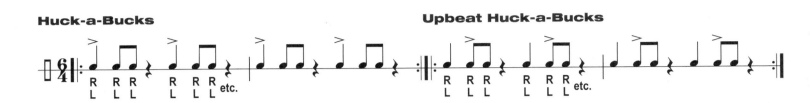

Huck-a-Bucks (Eighths to Sixteenths)

Upbeat Huck-a-Bucks (Eighths to Sixteenths)

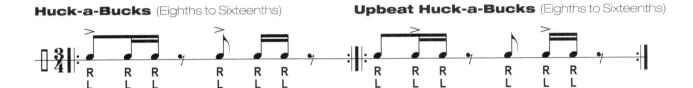

Swing Huck-a-Bucks

Upbeat Swing Huck-a-Bucks

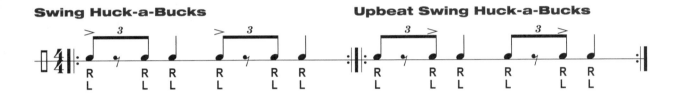

Huck-a-Bucks (Double Stops)

Upbeat Huck-a-Bucks (Double Stops)

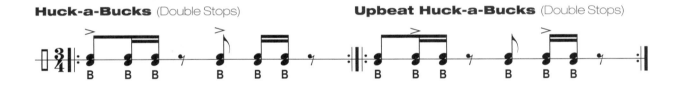

Swing Huck-a-Bucks (Double Stops)

Upbeat Swing Huck-a-Bucks (Double Stops)

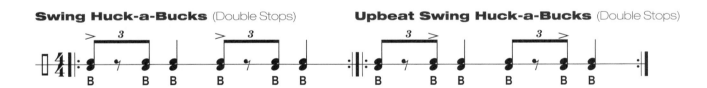

Huck-a-Bucks Mix — Hip-Hop Track 29

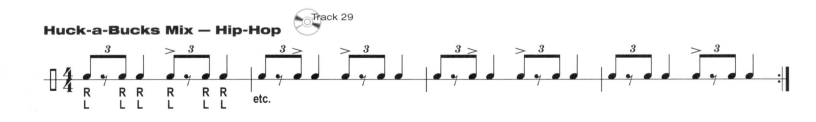

Double Huck-a-Bucks (Eighths to Sixteenths)

Double Huck-a-Bucks (Triplets)

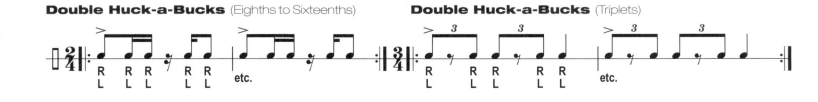

accent to double stroke (hands separate continued)

Upbeat Double Huck-a-Bucks
(Eighths to Sixteenths)

Double Huck-a-Bucks
(Triplets)

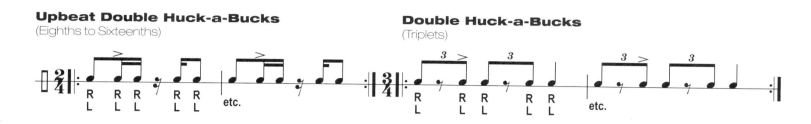

Two-Accent Huck-a-Bucks
(Eighths to Sixteenths)

Double Huck-a-Bucks
(Triplets)

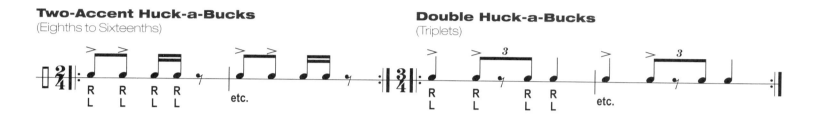

7/4 Huck-a-Bucks

Track 30

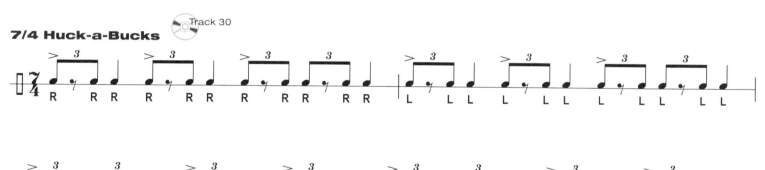

7/8 Huck-a-Bucks

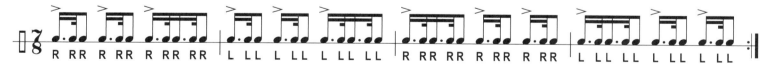

accent to double/drag builders (independence approach)

Focus Concepts

1. The first measure in the following group of exercises is the "hands-separate" pattern of common drag figures. The "hands-separate" pattern remains constant throughout and should look, feel and sound the same when the hands play together.
2. Keep the accent to double heights and sound consistent while adding the unaccented taps in the opposite hand.

Drags (Eighths to Sixteenths)

Track 31

Drags (Sixteenths to 32nds)

accent to double/drag builders (independence approach continued)

Drags (Triplets)

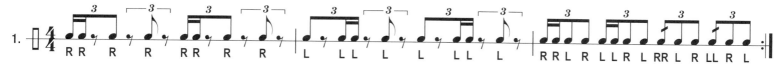

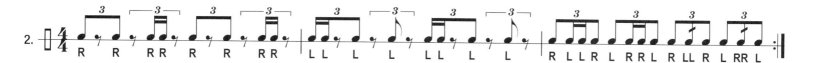

accent to double/roll builders (independence approach)

Five-Stroke Roll Builder

Six-Stroke Roll Builder

Seven-Stroke Roll Builder

Nine-Stroke Roll Builder

Ten-Stroke Roll Builder

accent to double/roll builders (independence approach continued)

Eleven-Stroke Roll Builder

Thirteen-Stroke Roll Builder

Fifteen-Stroke Roll Builder

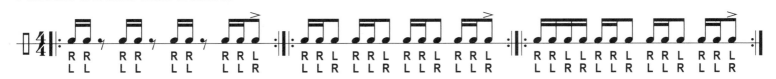

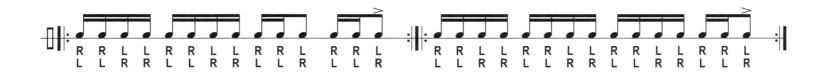

Seventeen-Stroke Roll Builder

accent to double/paradiddle builders (independence approach)

accent to double/paradiddle builders (independence approach continued)

Triple-Paradiddle Builder

Triple Paradiddle

Double-Paradiddle (one accent) Builder

Track 34

accent to double/paradiddle builders (independence approach continued)

Triple-Paradiddle (one accent) Builder

RRRRR R R R etc.
L L L LL L L L

RLRRR R R R   RRRRR R R R
LRLLL L L L   LLLL L L L

RLRLR RR R R R   RRRRR R R R
LRLRL LL L L L   LLLL L L L

RLRLRLRR R R R   RRRRR R R R
LRLRLRLL L L L   LLLL L L L

RLRLRLRRLR R R   RRRRR R R R
LRLRLRLLRL L L   LLLL L L L

RLRLRLRRLRLR R   RRRRR R R R
LRLRLRLLRLRL L   LLLL L L L

RLRLRLRRLRLRLR   RRRRR R R R
LRLRLRLLRLRLRL   LLLL L L L

RLRLRLRRLRLRLRL   RRRRR R R R
LRLRLRLLRLRLRLR   LLLL L L L

Triple Paradiddle

RLRLRLRRLRLRLRLL   R R R RR R R   RLRLRLRRLRLRLRLL
LRLRLRLLRLRLRLRR   L L L LL L L   LRLRLRLLRLRLRLRR

accent to double (independence exercises)

Independence Building (Ostinato & Quarter Notes)

Independence Building (Ostinato & Eighth Notes)

Independence Building (Ostinato & Sixteenth Notes)

Independence Building (Triplets — Single Notes)

Independence Building (Triplets — Two Notes)

Track 35

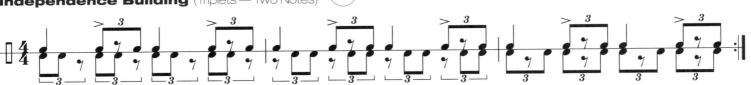

Focus Concepts

1. Observe strict heights in the ostinato hand while the opposite hand is mono-height.
2. Play, reversing the hand-rhythm assignments.

accent to double strokes (paradiddle chop-building combinations)

Single Paradiddle Chop Builder — Hands Separate

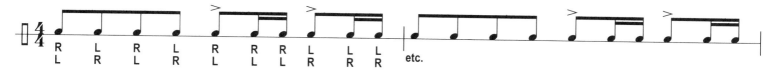

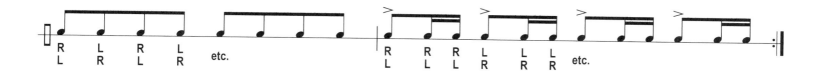

Single Paradiddle Chop Builder — Hands Together

Double Paradiddle Chop Builder — Hands Separate

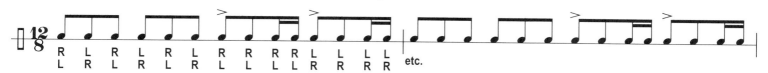

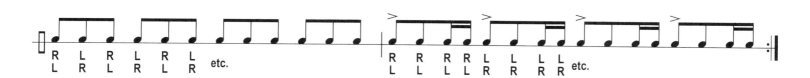

Double Paradiddle Chop Builder — Hands Together

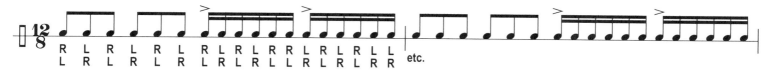

accent to double strokes (paradiddle chop-building combinations continued)

Triple Paradiddle Chop Builder — Hands Separate

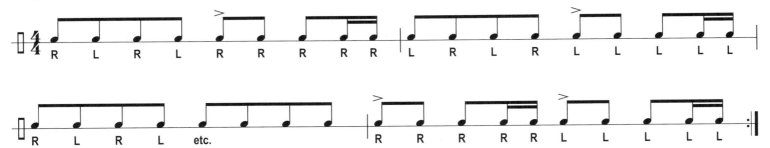

Triple Paradiddle Chop Builder — Hands Together

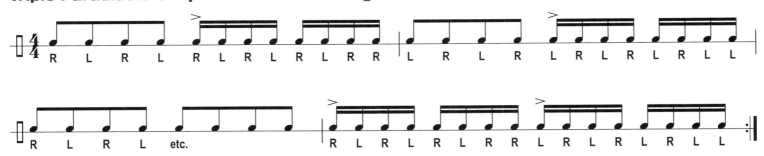

Paradiddle-Diddle Chop Builder — Hands Separate

Track 36

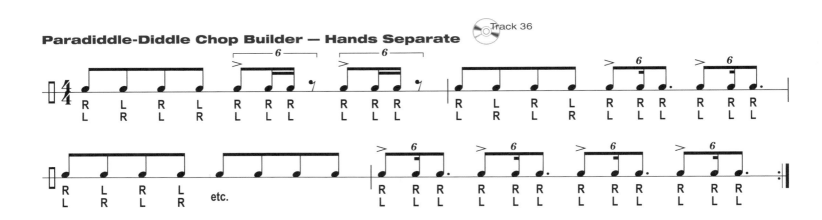

Paradiddle-Diddle Chop Builder — Hands Together

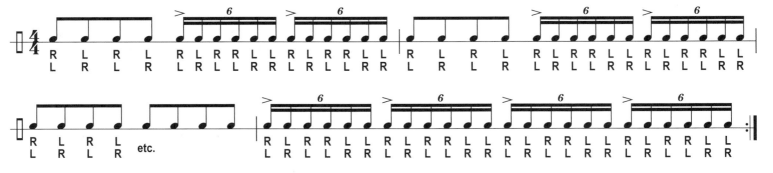

accent to double strokes (paradiddle chop-building combinations continued)

The Paradiddle Pyramid

```
R L R R L R L L    etc.
L R L L R L R R
```

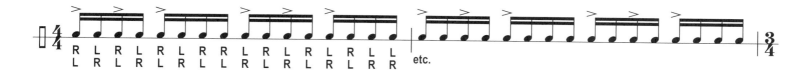

```
R L R L R L R R L R L R L R L L    etc.
L R L R L R L L R L R L R L R R
```

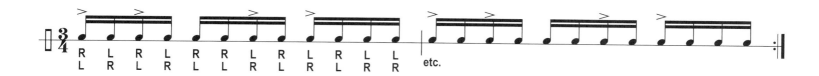

```
R L R L R R L R L R L R L L    etc.
L R L R L L R L R L R L R R
```

The Paradiddle Pyramid (One Accent)

```
R L R R L R L L    etc.
L R L L R L R R
```

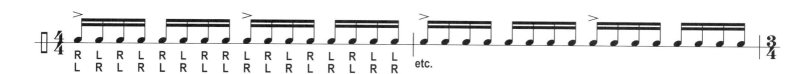

```
R L R L R L R R L R L R L R L L    etc.
L R L R L R L L R L R L R L R R
```

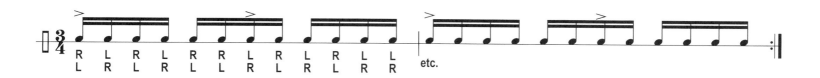

```
R L R L R R L R L R L R L L    etc.
L R L R L L R L R L R L R R
```

The Paradiddle-Diddle Burner (Eighths to Sixteenths)   Track 37

1.

```
R L R L    etc.        R L    R L R R L L R L R L R R L L R L R R    L L R L R R L L R    L
L R L R              L R    L R L L R R L R L R L L R R L R L L    R R L R L L R R L    R
```

2.

```
R L R L    etc.        R L    R L R R L L R L R L R R L L R L R R    L L R L R R L L R    L
L R L R              L R    L R L L R R L R L R L L R R L R L L    R R L R L L R R L    R
```

accent to double strokes (the grids)

The next eight exercises apply the grid exercises from the Accented Single-Stroke Section to Drags (accent to doubles). Although the drag is only shown on the first note of each grouping, these exercises should be practiced with the drag isolated on each beat of the grouping. Keep the accent scheme, but move the drag. Practice with a metronome, count quarter notes out loud and tap your foot on quarter notes while practicing.

Track 38

Triplet Grid — Forward

4's

R L R L R L
L R L R L R etc.

2's

R L R L R L
L R L R L R etc.

1's

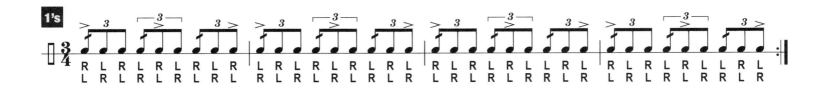

R L R L R L R L R L   L R L R L R L R L R   R L R L R L L L R L   R L R L R L L L R L
L R L R L R L R L R   R L R L R L R L R L   L R L R L R R R L R   L R L R L R R R L R

Sixteenth-Note Grid — Forward

4's

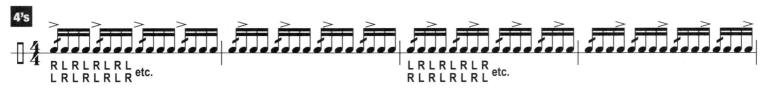

R L R L R L R L etc.
L R L R L R L R

L R L R L R L R etc.
R L R L R L R L

2's

R L R L R L R L etc.
L R L R L R L R

L R L R L R L R etc.
R L R L R L R L

1's

R L R L R L R L etc.
L R L R L R L R

accent to double strokes (the grids continued)

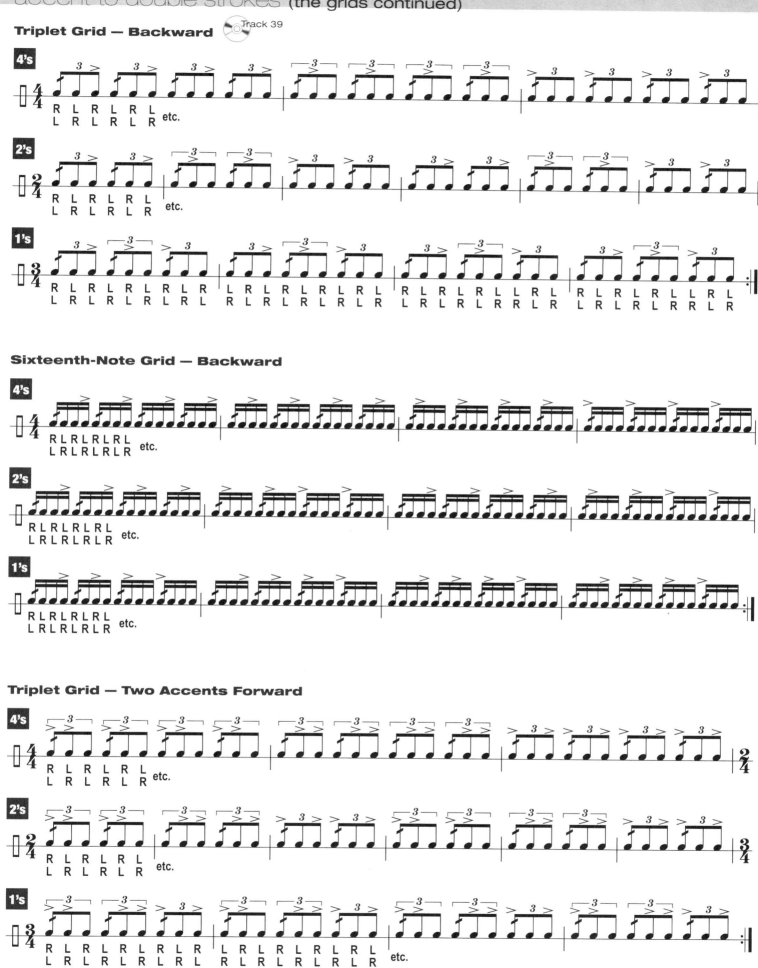

accent to double strokes (the grids continued)

Sixteenth-Note Grid — Two Accents Forward

4's

RLRLRLRL
LRLRLRLR etc.

2's

RLRLRLRL
LRLRLRLR etc.

1's

RLRLRLRL
LRLRLRLR etc.

Triplet Grid — Two Accents Backward

4's

R L R L R L
L R L R L R etc.

2's

R L R L R L
L R L R L R etc.

1's

RLRLRLRLR
LRLRLRLRL etc.

LRLRLRLRL
RLRLRLRLR etc.

Sixteenth-Note Grid — Two Accents Backward

4's

RLRLRLRL
LRLRLRLR etc.

2's

RLRLRLRL
LRLRLRLR etc.

1's

RLRLRLRL
LRLRLRLR etc.

accented double strokes (drumset application — time functioning)

Half-Time Shuffle with Double Paradiddle Combination Track 40

R L R L R R L R L R L L R L R L R R L R L R L L etc.

Samba Pattern with Accents Track 41

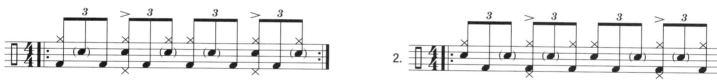

Try reversing the hands with the samba pattern.

Independence Building with Triplets (Doubles/Jazz-Time Variations) Track 42

1.    2.

3.    4.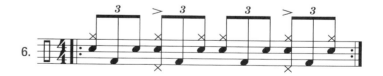

5.    6.

7. 8.

accented double strokes (drumset application — solos and fills)

Eighth-Note Paradiddles — RH Lead *Track 43*

R L R R L R L L R L R R L R L L

Eighth-Note Paradiddles — LH Lead

L R L L R L R R L R L L R L R R

**Eighth-Note Paradiddles —
LH Lead Around the Drums** *Track 44*

L R L L R L R R

**Eighth-Note Paradiddles —
RH Lead Around the Drums**

R L R R L R L L

Paradiddles with Triplets — RH Clockwise *Track 45*

R L R R L R L L R L R R L R L L L R L L R L R R L R L L R L R R

Paradiddles with Triplets — LH Counterclockwise

L R L L R L R R L R L L R L R R R L R R L R L L R L R R L R L L

Paradiddle-Diddles with Triplets — RH Clockwise *Track 46*

R L R R L R L L R L R R L R L L R L R R L R L L R L R R L R L L

Paradiddle-Diddles with Triplets — LH Counterclockwise

L R L L R L R R L R L L R L R R L R L L R L R R L R L L R L R R

Paradiddle-Diddles with Sixteenths — RH Clockwise *Track 47*

R L R R L R L L R L R R L R L L R L R R L L R L R R L L R L R R L L R L R R

Paradiddle-Diddles with Sixteenths — LH Counterclockwise

L R L L R L R R L R L L R L R R L R L L R R L R L L R R L R L L R R L L R R L

Chapter 3
Buzz & Multiple Bounce Rolls

buzz, multiple-bounce & orchestral roll builders (hands separate)

Closed Roll Builder #1

Focus Concepts

1. Allow each stroke to bounce for as long as possible.
2. Pay attention to the amount of squeeze at the fulcrum (between the thumb and index finger) used for each length.
3. Avoid the temptation to remove your middle finger.
4. Practice the following exercise at all dynamic levels, especially pianissimo.

Closed Roll Builder #2 — The Pressed Roll

Focus Concepts

1. Again, allow each stick to bounce as long as possible within the given rhythm of the "skeleton." In playing rolls, the rhythmic hand speed is referred to as a "skeleton." For example, sixteenth notes are used as the "roll skeleton" in measure 4 of this exercise.
2. Although sometimes notated with slashes through the stem, some contemporary scores delineate "closed, buzz, concert or orchestral rolls" with a "z" through the stem. Traditionally, this notation system was not used so a roll interpretation (being either open or closed) depends on the performance situation. Most rolls in orchestral and concert band situations are closed, while most in marching or rudimental situations are open.

Both Hands in Unison (Double Stops)

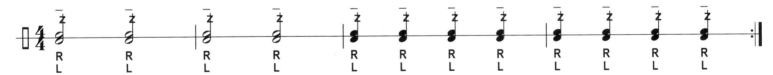

Lengthening the Buzz (Experiment with Fulcrum Pressure)

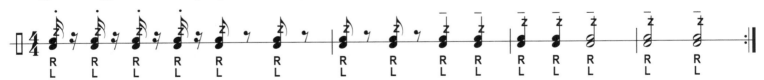

Focus Concepts

1. When playing this exercise, start by pressing the bead of the stick into the head to produce a short buzz length.
2. As you start to lengthen the buzz, notice that you decrease the pressure on the beads to make the stick bounce longer.

Track 48

Closed Roll Builder #3 — Overlapping the Buzz

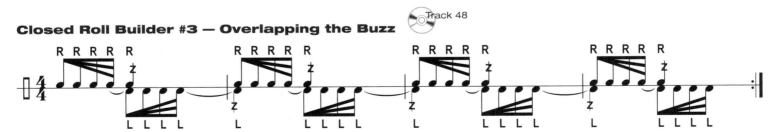

This exercise is similar to #1, except you must overlap the start of each hand in order to make the roll appear "seamless."

closed roll builders (independence approach — duple)

Closed Roll Builder (Duple)

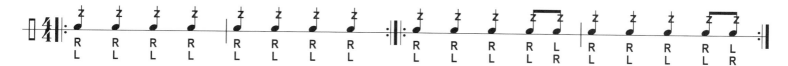

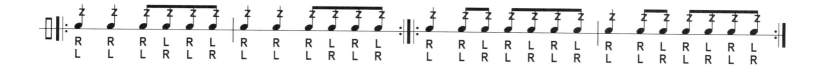

closed roll builders (independence approach — triple)

Closed Roll Builder (Triplets)

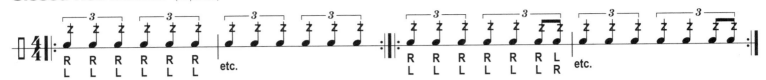

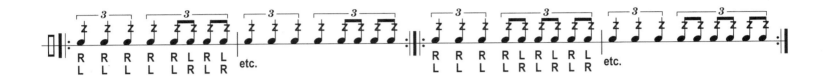

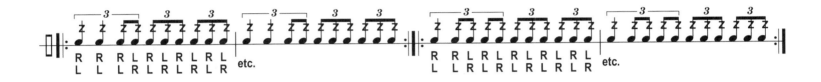

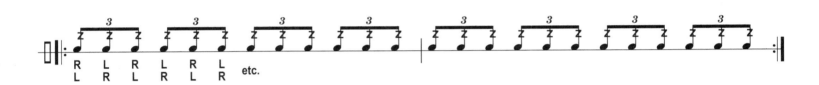

Closed Roll Builder in 6/8

closed roll builders

Major Technical Approaches with Closed Rolls

1. **Pressed Rolls** – Buzz each hand precisely for the duration of each stroke in the roll skeleton. Used primarily for pianissimo to mezzo forte.
2. **Overlapping** – Start the next stroke in the roll while the opposite hand is still buzzing. Make it seamless. Used primarily for pianissimo to mezzo piano.
3. **Triple-Stroke Rolls** – A controlled bounce of three notes on each hand. The stick is lifted after it strikes the drum for the third time. This technique is used to achieve louder orchestral rolls, forte and louder.

Practice these approaches with the next set of skeleton exercises.

Closed Roll Builder (Duple & Triple Skeletons)

1.
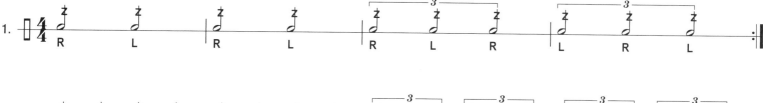

2.

3.
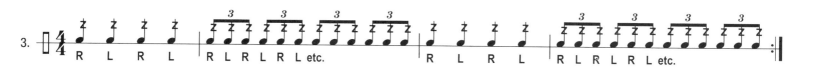

4.
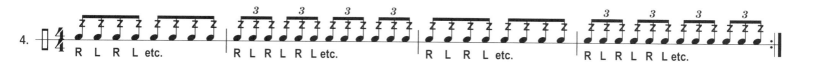

5.

6.
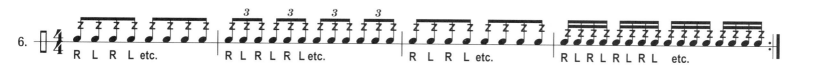

7.

8.

closed roll builders

 Focus Concepts

1. Often times for closed rolls, odd-grouping skeletons are preferred because they give the player a sense of equal weight for each hand in a sustain.
2. Although sustained closed rolls are often referred to as "unmeasured" in terms of a rhythmic skeleton, getting familiar with the following odd groupings can give the player greater facility in performing even, consistent and smooth rolls.

Closed Roll Builders (Odd-Grouping Skeletons)

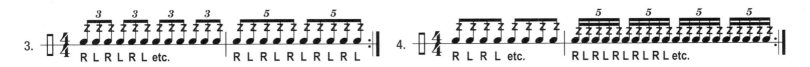

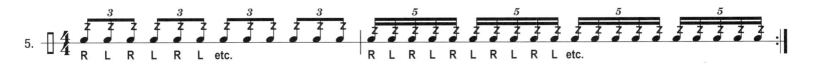

closed roll builders

Closed Roll Builders (Odd-Grouping Skeletons Continued)

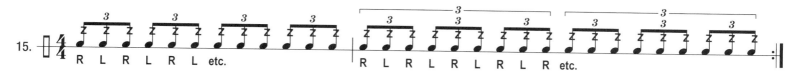

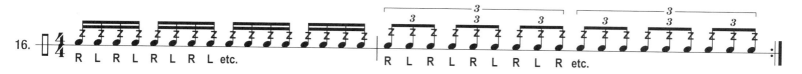

Track 49

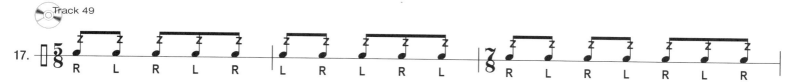

applying all multiple-bounce concepts

The following exercise, shared with me by Dr. Robert Bridge, is among the trickiest to perform both smoothly and expressively. Applying all "three technical approaches," plus choosing and changing to appropriate skeletons for the musical requirements, help make this exercise one of the most challenging to master.

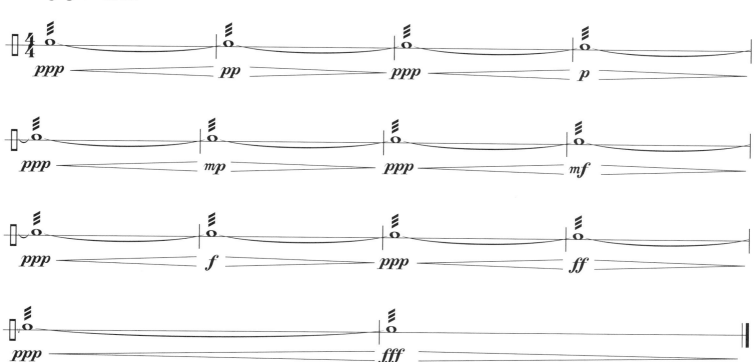

rolls in marches

It's important to remember that when performing in orchestra, concert band, wind ensemble, percussion ensemble and most chamber music situations, that nearly all the written rolls should be played as closed rolls.

Concert Band Notation　　　　　　　　　　　　　**Concert Band Interpretation**

Although it is ultimately up to the conductor, the following are roll suggestions (shared with me by John R. Beck) for ensemble marches. Please keep in mind that the buzzed suggestions could be played with double strokes (open rolls) at the conductor's or player's discretion. In the following examples, the terms *fast* and *moderate* refer to tempo.

Fast (duple feel) Notation　　　　　　　　　　**Fast (duple feel) Interpretation**

Moderate (triple feel) Notation　　　　　　　**Moderate (triple feel) Interpretation**

Moderate Notation (swing or backbeat feel)　　**Moderate (swing or backbeat feel) Interpretation**

Fast 6/8 Notation　　　　　　　　　　　　　**Fast 6/8 Interpretation**

Moderate 6/8 Notation　　　　　　　　　　　**Moderate 6/8 Interpretation**

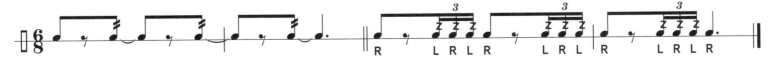

closed rolls (roll chart)

The Five-Stroke Roll

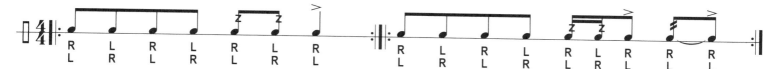

The Six-Stroke Roll

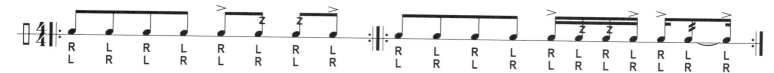

The Seven-Stroke Roll

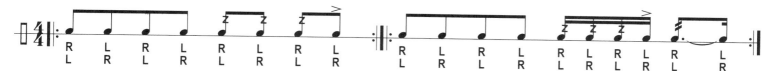

The Nine-Stroke Roll

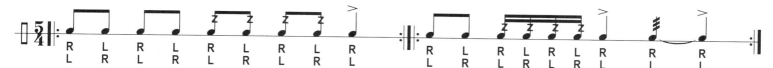

The Ten-Stroke Roll

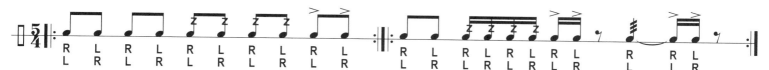

The Eleven-Stroke Roll

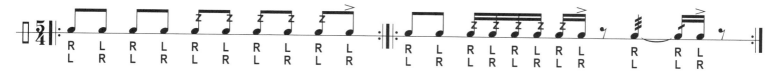

The Thirteen-Stroke Roll

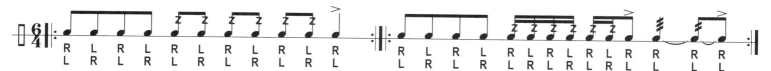

The Fifteen-Stroke Roll

The Seventeen-Stroke Roll

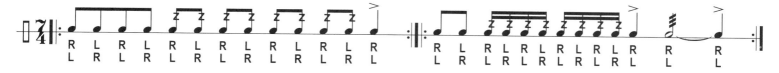

buzz rolls (drumset application — time functioning)

Rock Pattern

Samba Pattern Track 50

Tango Pattern Track 51

Chapter 4
Drags

the drag (from the 40 official PAS international rudiments)

Eighth to Sixteenth

Sixteenth to 32nd

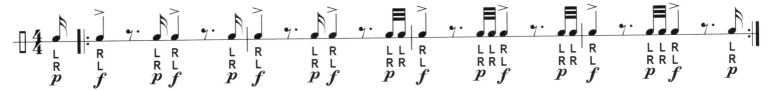

Sixteenth to 32nd — Alternating

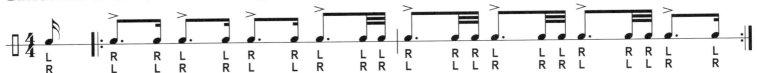

Focus Concepts

1. Start with the drag note low and the primary stroke high.
2. Keep the double stroke even by emphasizing the second stroke of the drag figure.

drags — concert and rudimental interpretation

It is important to remember when performing in orchestra, concert band, wind ensemble, percussion ensemble, and most chamber music situations that nearly all the written drags are usually played as closed or buzzed. There are some orchestral players who interpret these figures as open (exactly two notes). In a concert situation (except for marches), I recommend playing them closed. Although it is ultimately up to the conductor, the drags could be interpreted as either closed or open. Both ways are presented below.

Concert Band/ Orchestral Notation   **Closed Interpretation**   **Open Interpretation**

drags (concert and rudimental interpretation continued)

In a rudimental performance, drags are almost always performed open. The notation of drags in traditional rudimental solos, such as those by Charley Wilcoxon, have rhythmic ambiguity and are often difficult to read at first. I recommend the following method for reading rudimental solos that are written with drags as ornaments. In your mind's eye, convert the ornament to the sixteenth note (in most cases) before the note the ornament is tied to. While this is not the last word in interpreting the figure, it provides a rhythmic framework for the drag that can then be modified to fit the style and taste of the performer. I call this the "Rudimental Drag Rule," although it might also be helpful when initially interpreting some challenging concert drag passages.

Traditional Rudimental Notation

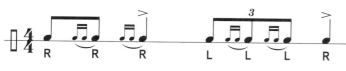

Applying "The Rudimental Drag Rule"

Traditional Rudimental Notation in 6/8

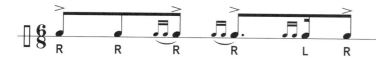

Applying "The Rudimental Drag Rule" in 6/8

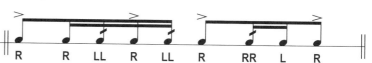

Traditional Rudimental Notation

Applying "The Rudimental Drag Rule"

Traditional Rudimental Notation in 6/8

Applying "The Rudimental Drag Rule" in 6/8

Traditional Rudimental Notation in Fast 3

Applying "The Rudimental Drag Rule" in Fast 3

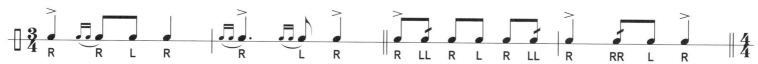

drag rudiment exercises (skeleton approach)

Alternating Drags — Rudimental Interpretation

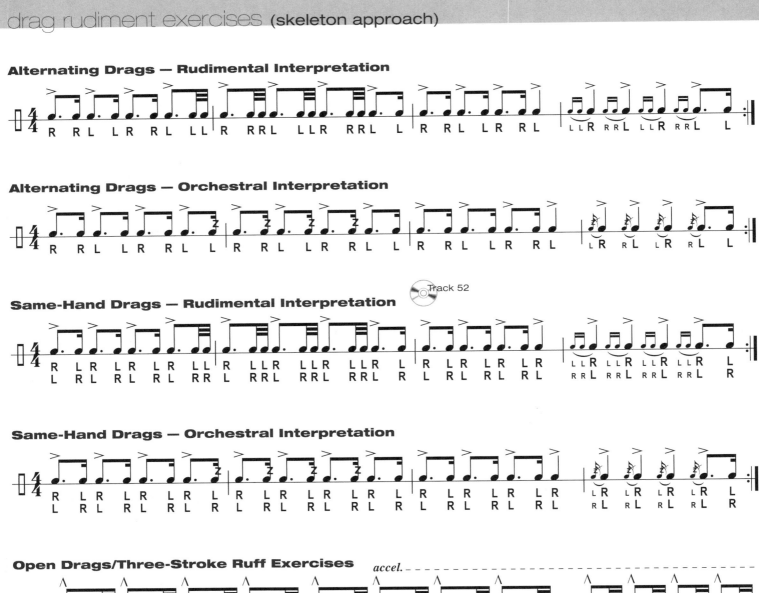

Alternating Drags — Orchestral Interpretation

Track 52

Same-Hand Drags — Rudimental Interpretation

Same-Hand Drags — Orchestral Interpretation

Open Drags/Three-Stroke Ruff Exercises

four-stroke ruff exercises

Besides alternating a four-stroke ruff, there are different sticking options that can be employed. The next set of exercises works on two of the most popular choices, especially for softer dynamics: RRL and RLL (their inverse LLR and LRR can also be practiced).

Focus Concepts
1. Keep the exact two heights: accent to grace notes.
2. Make the rhythm perfect by focusing on the triplet in the end of each grouping.
3. The right and left hand grace notes must match each other perfectly for the articulation of the ornament to be clear and audible.

Exercise #1 (RRL) Track 53   **Orchestral Notation**

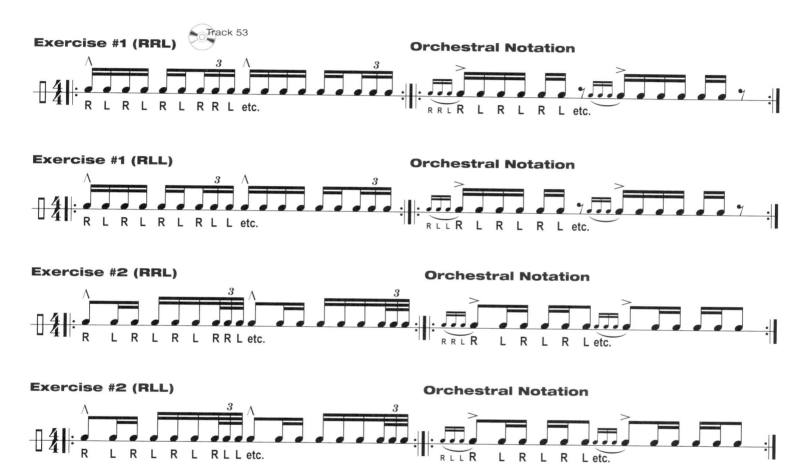

single-drag tap (skeleton approach) Track 54

Single-Drag Tap (Rudimental Interpretation)

single-drag tap (skeleton approach continued)

Single-Drag Tap (Orchestral Interpretation)

double-drag tap (skeleton approach)

Double-Drag Tap (Rudimental Interpretation)

Double-Drag Tap (Orchestral Interpretation)

Track 55

Double-Drag Tap (Alternate Notation — Rudimental Interpretation)

lesson 25 (hands-separate approach)

Lesson 25 (Rudimental Interpretation) Track 56

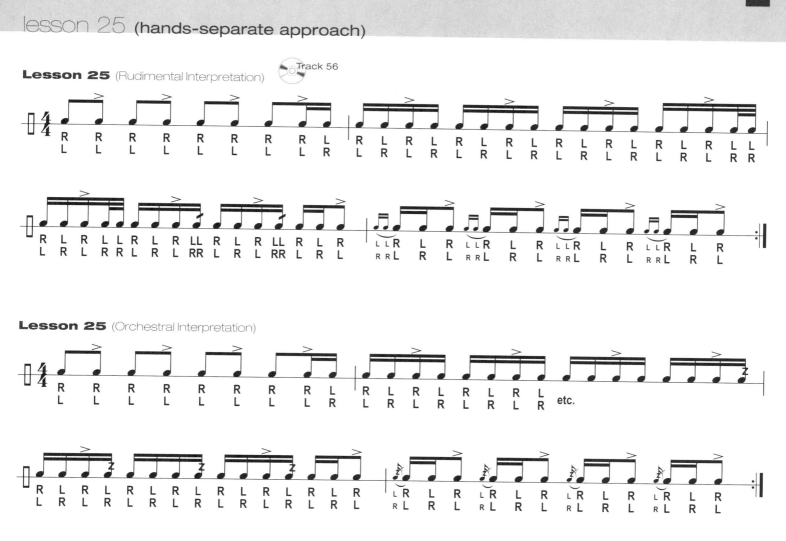

single dragaddile (hands separate approach)

Single Dragadiddle (Rudimental Interpretation — Eighths to Sixteenths)

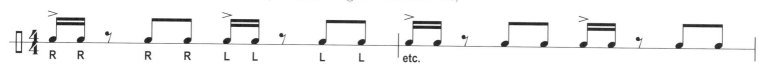

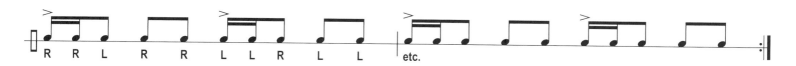

Single Dragadiddle (Rudimental Interpretation — Sixteenths to 32nds) Track 57

drag paradiddle #1 (hands-separate approach)

Drag Paradiddle #1 (Rudimental Interpretation) Track 58

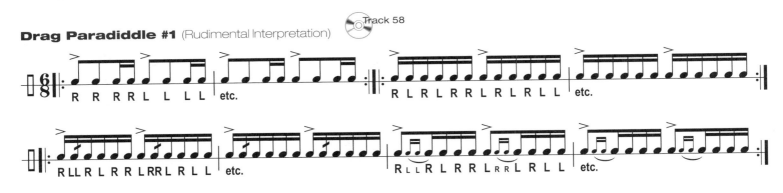

drag paradiddle #2 (hands separate approach)

Drag Paradiddle #2 (Rudimental Interpretation) Track 59

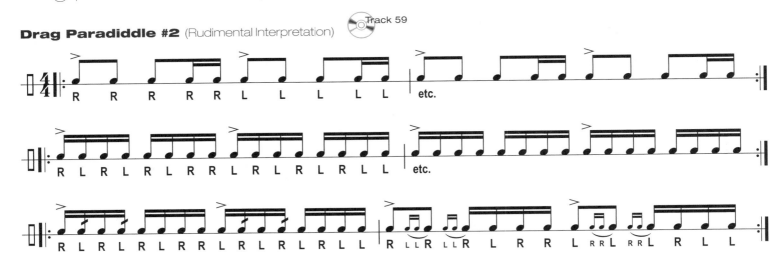

single ratamacue (skeleton approach)

Single Ratamacue (Rudimental Interpretation)

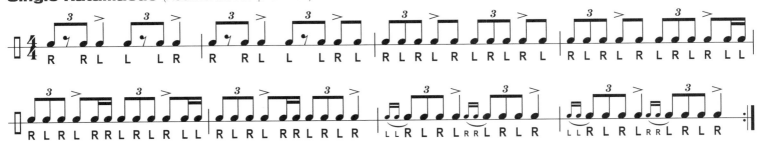

Single Ratamacue (Rudimental Interpretation — Alternate Notation)

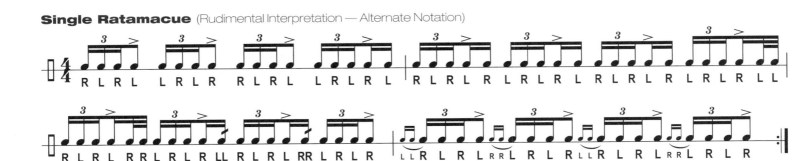

double ratamacue (skeleton approach)

Double Ratamacue (Rudimental Interpretation)

Double Ratamacue (Rudimental Interpretation — Alternate Notation)

Triple Ratamacue (Rudimental Interpretation)

triple ratamacue (skeleton approach)

Triple Ratamacue (Rudimental Interpretation — Alternate Notation)

R   R   R L R L   L   L   L R L R | R   R   R L R L   L   L   L R L R

R L R L R L R L   R L R L R L R L | R L R L R L R L   R L R L R L R L L

R L L R L L R L R L   R R L R R L R R L R L R L L | R L R L R L R L R L R L R L R L R

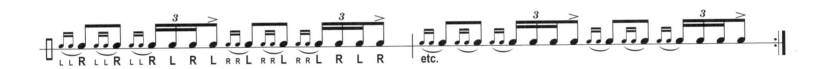

LL R LL R LL R L R L   R R L R R L R R L R L R | etc.

drag rudiments (drumset application — fills and solos)

Drag Rudiment Applied to Fills #1   **Drag Rudiment Applied to Fills #2**

Drag Rudiment Applied to Fills #3   **Drag Rudiment Applied to Fills — Two-Bar Phrase**

Lesson 25 Applied to Fills — Two-Bar Phrase

Lesson 25 Applied to Fills — Triplets

Drag Rudiment Applied to Fills — Triplets

Ratamacue Applied to Fills #1   **Ratamacue Applied to Fills #2**

drag rudiments (drumset application — fills and solos continued)

Track 67

Ratamacue Applied to Fills — Combining #1 and #2

Track 68

Ratamacue Applied to Fills — Two-Bar Phrase

Chapter 5
Flams

the flam rudiments (hands-separate approach)

Flams and Grace Note Interpretation

It should be noted that exact rhythmic interpretation of the hands-separate patterns produce double-stops, not flams. The exercises are designed to develop muscle control and the independence needed to execute flam rudiments regardless of grace note interpretation. Proper mastery of the exercises will allow the performer advanced control of the unaccented notes. This control can be manipulated

to practice the flam rudiments in all types of grace note interpretations, from extremely open or wide grace notes to tight, almost double stop (flat flam) grace notes.

Be sure to practice all the exercises starting with the left hand playing the ostinato. Some flam rudiments are symmetrical (both hands execute the same rhythm during the performance of the rudiment).

symmetrical flam rudiments

Alternating Flams (Hands-Separate Approach) Track 69

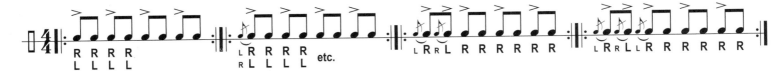

Focus Concepts

1. Start with the grace note low and the primary stroke high.
2. The ostinato hand (first bar) should be playing "bucks" throughout the entire exercise.
3. Be sure to play the entire exercise with the left hand playing the ostinato.

symmetrical flam rudiments (continued)

The Flam Accent (Hands-Separate Approach)   Track 70

Focus Concepts

1. Start with the taps low and the primary stroke high.
2. The ostinato hand (first bar) should continue throughout the entire exercise.
3. Be sure to play the entire exercise with the left hand playing the ostinato.

The Flam Tap (Hands-Separate Approach)   Track 71

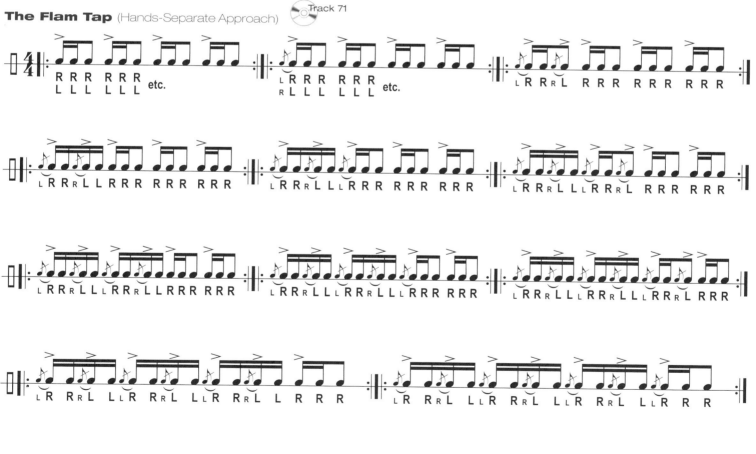

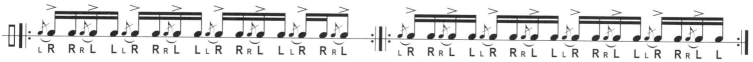

symmetrical flam rudiments (continued)

The Flam Paradiddle (Hands-Separate Approach) Track 72

The Single-Flammed Mill (Hands-Separate Approach) Track 73

symmetrical flam rudiments (continued)

The Flam Drag (Hands-Separate Approach)   Track 74

The Flam Stutter or "Cheese" (Hands-Separate Approach)   Track 75

The Flam Five-Stroke Roll or "Flam Fives" (Hands-Separate Approach)   Track 76

symmetrical flam rudiments (continued)

The Invert Motion

Some symmetrical flam rudiments, like the inverted flam tap, flam paradiddle-diddle, or the asymmetrical pata fla-fla, utilize the invert motion. This movement can be more challenging to control and execute because the accent comes quickly after a tap with very little rhythmic space in which to lift the stick. The next exercise breaks down the inverted flam-tap, illustrating the invert motion. This motion should be isolated and practiced everyday for chop building and maintenance.

The Inverted Flam Tap (Hands-Separate Approach) ◯ Track 77

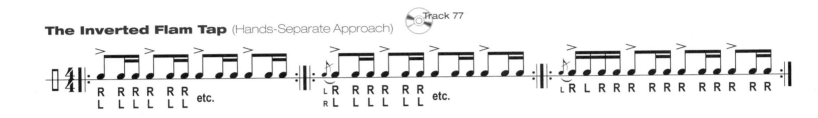

symmetrical flam rudiments (continued)

The Flam Paradiddle-Diddle (Hands-Separate Approach) Track 78

asymmetrical flam rudiments

Some flam rudiments are asymmetrical, such as the flamacue illustrated in the next exercise. Asymmetrical means the hands are playing different rhythms or motions. Except for the accent, the Swiss Army Triplet could arguably fit in either the symmetrical or asymmetrical category.

The Flamacue (Hands-Separate Approach)   Track 79

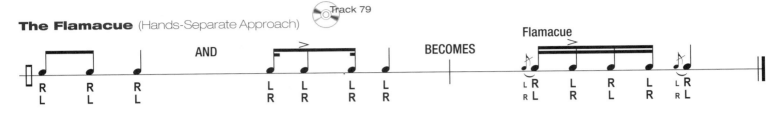

The Flamacue Built from the Unaccented Hand

The Flamacue Built from The Accented Hand

The Swiss Army Triplet (Hands-Separate Approach)   Track 80

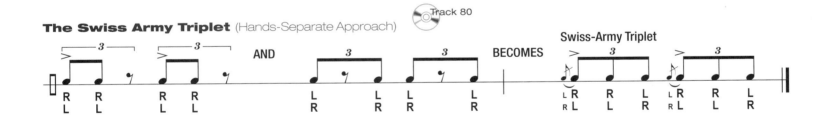

The Swiss Army Triplets Built from the Unaccented Hand

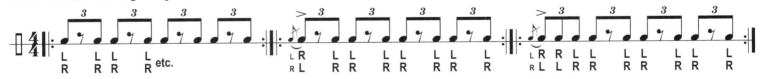

asymmetrical flam rudiments (continued)

The Swiss Army Triplets Built from the Accented Hand

The Pataflafla (Hands-Separate Approach)

Track 81

The Pataflafla Built from the "Invert Motion"

The Pataflafla Built from the "Accent To Double" Stroke

flam rudiments (the grids)

Practice the following four exercises as written (with flams on the downbeat), then move the flams to the second and third note in the triplets and the second, third and fourth in the sixteenth grids. Also practice applying Flam Drags, Cheeses and Flam Fives on the triplet grids. Practice with a metronome and count quarter notes out loud while playing these accent schemes. Tap your foot on quarter notes, as well.

Triplet Grid — Forward

Sixteenth-Note Grid — Forward

flam rudiments (the grids continued)

Triplet Grid — Backward

4's

R L R L R L etc.
L R L R L R

2's

R L R L R L etc.
L R L R L R

1's

R L R L R L R L R etc.
L R L R L R L R L

Sixteenth-Note Grid — Backward

4's

R L R L R L R L etc.
L R L R L R L R

2's

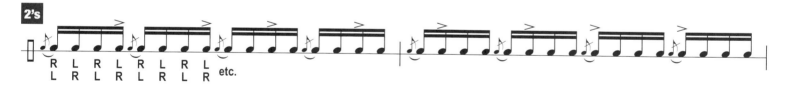

R L R L R L R L etc.
L R L R L R L R

1's

R L R L R L R L etc.
L R L R L R L R

flam rudiments (drumset application — fills & solos)

Track 82

The Flam Tap Applied to Fills #1   **The Flam Applied to Fills**

Track 83

Track 84

The Flam Tap Applied to Fills #2   **Flam Taps Played as Double Stops (Flat Flams)**

Track 85

Flam Taps Applied to Fills — Triplets #1

Flam Taps Applied to Fills — Triplets #2   **Flam Taps Applied to Fills — Triplets #3**

Track 86

Swiss Army Triplets Fill Ideas (à la Tony Williams)

Flam Taps Applied to Fills — Two-Bar Phrase

snare and bass drum practical independence

With the independence gained through the exercises in this book, apply the strokes to produce common grooves and variations contained in the following three pages. Be sure to master the different hi-hat and ride cymbal ostinato patterns in the right hand. For added independence, reverse the hands playing the hi-hat ostinato with the left hand and the right hand on the snare. After you master the grooves with the right hand, left hand and right foot (BD), move your ostinato hand to the ride cymbal and add the left foot ("stepped") hi-hat rhythms to work on four-limb independence.

Also play the next 42 patterns with the following hi-hat/ride-cymbal *ostinati*.

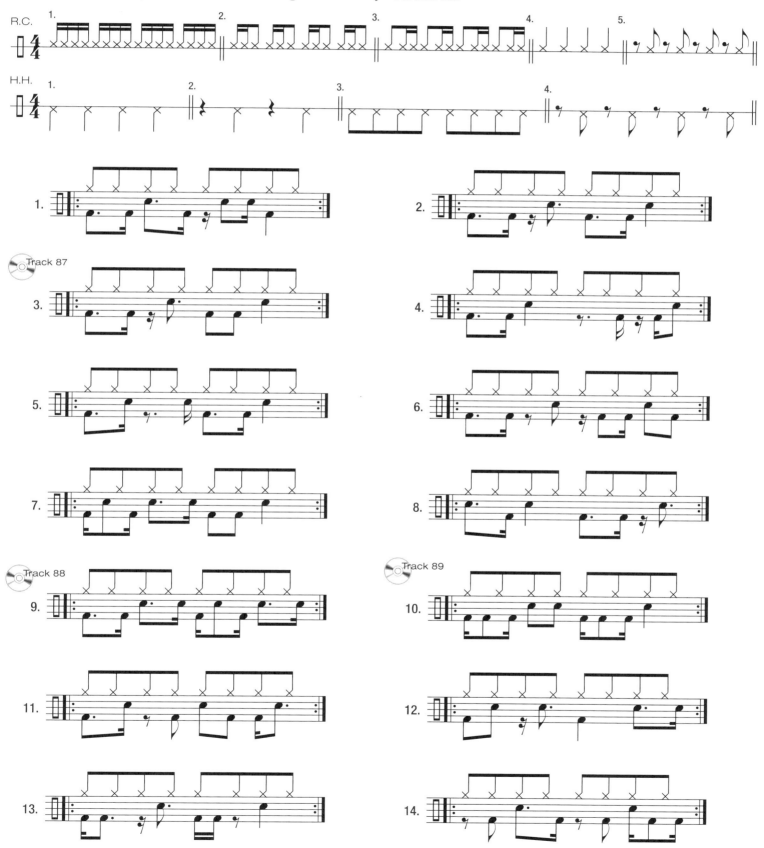

snare and bass drum practical independence

15.

16.

17.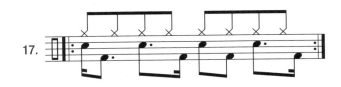

18.

19.

20.

21.

22.

Track 90

23.

24.

25.

26.

27.

28.

snare and bass drum practical independence

Half-Time Feel

29.

30.

31.

32.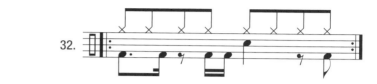

Track 91

33.

Track 92

34.

35.

36.

37.

38.

39.

40.

41.

42.

Jeff wrote the book on snare playing.
And here are a few of the sticks that helped him do it.

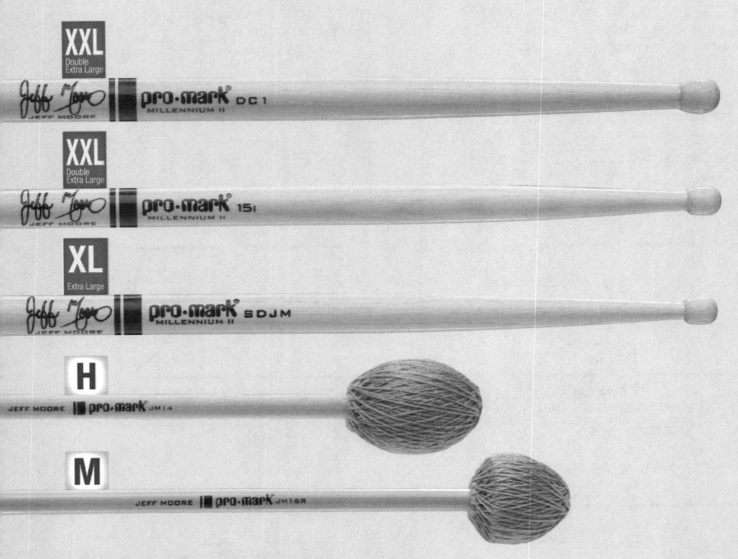

Jeff's redesigned Autograph keyboard mallets are lighter and longer and are designed for optimun sound enhancement. Available in 7 tones.